Love to Sew

Mug Rugs

For instructions on how to make the mug rug shown above, see page 14; instructions for the mug rug shown opposite are on page 30.

Love to Sew

Mug Rugs

Christa Rolf

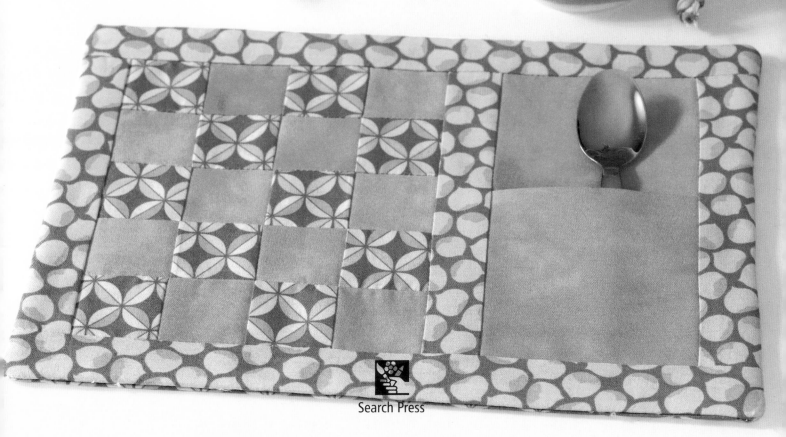

Search Press

First published in Great Britain 2013 by Search Press Limited
Wellwood, North Farm Road, Tunbridge Wells, Kent TN2 3DR

Reprinted 2013, 2014 (twice), 2015

Original German edition published as *Mug Rugs*

Copyright © 2012 Christophorus Verlag GmbH,
Freiburg/Germany

English translation by Burravoe Translation Services

ISBN: 978-1-84448-926-8

Designs and production: Renate Bieber, Bea Galler,
Sabine Günther, Peggy Donda-Kobert, Petra
Herbrechtsmeier, Regine Joskowiak, Beate Mazek,
Veronika Mickenhagen-Cox, Beate Pöhlamm, Kerstin Porsch,
Susanne Rosensträter, Ulla Stewart, Verena Surerus,
Andreas Wolf, Heike Ziefuß

Photography: Uwe Blick

Styling: Karin S. Schlag

Technical drawings and patterns: Susanne Nöllgen,
GrafikBüro Berlin

The manufacturers mentioned in this book refer to those
organisations that kindly supplied the materials and
equipment used by the author. Many of these organisations
provide on-line ordering facilities and distribute worldwide.
However, all of the materials and equipment used in this
book can be readily obtained from alternative sources,
including specialist stores, on-line suppliers and
mail-order companies.

Printed in China

Geometrics, page 13

Carpet of Flowers, page 16

A Treat for the Eyes, page 22

Monkeying Around , page 24

Sew Time, page 34

Pretty in Pink, page 36

Good Morning, page 46

Coffee Time, page 48

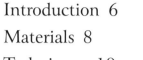

Contents

Prime Time, page 18

Samplers with Style, page 20

It's All in the Name, page 26

Tea for One, page 28

Pocket Rug, page 30

Flower Power, page 32

Baker's Shop, page 38

Two's Company, page 40

Hand-stitched Hexagons, page 42

Cathedral Windows, page 44

Creative Break, page 50

Out of Line, page 52

Nostalgic Charm, page 54

Christmas Landscape, page 56

Introduction

We all like to create a safe, comfortable environment in which we can feel relaxed and secure. Whether at home, away at university or in the workplace, one way of making our immediate environment more homely is with small, handmade items, such as the mug rugs featured in this book.

I have chosen a number of particularly charming mug rugs here to show how creativity can contribute to a comfortable and friendly ambience. All the designers are pleased to share their creations, which demonstrate a wealth of imagination and skill, so a huge 'thank you' to them!

I hope these ideas inspire you to design and make your own mug rugs, either by following the instructions for one of the projects shown here or by simply using this book as a springboard for creating something entirely your own. A mug rug will always be your own personal work of art, and will hopefully bring you tremendous pleasure, both in the making of it and in its use.

What is a mug rug?

A mug rug is exactly what it says – a small rug for your mug. A little larger than an ordinary coaster, it is perfect for putting under your favourite mug, and there's even space for a biscuit or two! Mug rugs are a great way to decorate the table when you're having a cosy get-together with friends; when a visitor pops in unexpectedly; or for a quick, informal meeting with work colleagues. Use a matching set of them for a small gathering, or spoil yourself and choose your favourite one for when you're on your own.

Mug rugs can be made in many different ways and from a variety of fabrics, and they do not have to be rectangular either – how about a house shape (page 38) or a coffee cup (page 48), for example? All you need to remember is that your mug rug will occasionally need washing. Apart from that, you can make it in any design, shape, material and colour you like – anything goes. And because a mug rug is quite small, it is never a daunting project.

This is an ideal opportunity to try out different patchwork techniques and appliqué work. You could even embroider or appliqué your name on your mug rug (see page 26), and add your favourite motifs. In addition to the ones in this book, you can find inspiration on the Internet or from children's colouring books, or you can even make up your own designs. You can then transfer your pattern to fabric and create your very own mug rug.

A single mug rug might look a little lonely on the breakfast table, so why not make a pair – or even a quartet of them? Using the same fabrics but different techniques is a great way to add variety to the table, and everyone can have their own personal favourite. The projects on pages 18, 24, 40 and 52 show how you might go about creating such a set.

So what is the best way to start? One idea is to take your favourite mug with you when you go to buy the fabric so you can choose one that matches it. You might also like to have a piece of paper in the size you want the mug rug to be, so you can sketch out a few designs. Alternatively, you could simply copy your favourite designs from this book exactly. Happy sewing!

Each project has been given a level of difficulty:

♡   *easy*

♡ ♡   *average*

♡ ♡ ♡   *more challenging*

Materials

Fabrics

Cotton fabrics are the easiest to use, but they may shrink when washed for the first time. Always press with a steam iron before using and preferably pre-wash them, particularly strong colours that may run in the first wash.

Wool felt

Wool felt has a very special charm and can be used in patchwork and for appliqué. It has the great advantage that the edges will not fray. Felt gives motifs a sculptural feel, and the slightly fluffy surface makes them look and feel very soft and delicate. Unlike craft felt, wool felt can be washed – which is essential for anything that goes on the table.

Wadding, webbing and stabiliser

- Wadding (batting) is used as a layer between the front and back of each mug rug. Lightweight wadding is sufficient for the projects in this book. Thin, heat-resistant wadding, such as Insul-Bright, is highly suitable.
- Fusible webbing, such as Vliesofix/Bondaweb or Pellon Wonder-Under, enables you to fix appliqués permanently simply by ironing the layers together (see page 11).
- Embroidery stabiliser is available in different forms to suit different needs, techniques and preferences. Tear-away embroidery stabiliser helps support fabric and feed it under the machine foot when working appliqué on a machine. It helps produce a neat, smooth finish. Embroidery backing for temporary use, such as Totally Stable by Gütermann Sulky, has only a slightly adhesive effect, and tears away completely when no longer required. This embroidery stabiliser is a great help with appliqués made of wool felt.

Cutting aids

- A rotary cutter has a smooth blade that cuts easily through several layers of fabric, and is a great help when cutting out fabrics for patchwork. The medium size (45mm/1¾in blade) is the best for beginners.
- A patchwork ruler made of transparent acrylic helps to cut out fabrics with absolute precision.
- Use the rotary cutter and patchwork ruler on a self-healing cutting mat. This protects your surfaces and the delicate rotary blade. A cutting mat, rotary cutter and ruler are often available as a set.

Marker pens

A water-soluble marker pen, such as Aqua Trickmarker by Prym, is ideal for transferring motifs or embroidery patterns on to textiles. The lines can be wiped away with a damp cloth or sponge.

Note

The fabric requirements in this book are based on a fabric width of 110cm (44in). However, sometimes you only need a small amount, in which case you can use remnants. Check the 'Cutting out' sections to see exactly what you need.

Techniques

Using templates

Trace or copy the pattern on to card or template plastic and cut out carefully along the outer line. Place the template on the wrong side of the fabric and draw the outline (sewing line) on to the fabric using a soft pencil or removable fabric marker pen. A seam allowance, usually 0.75cm (¼in), is required when sewing pieces together, although an allowance of only 0.5cm (⁵⁄₁₆in) is generally more advisable when sewing intricate shapes or tight curves. Either add the seam allowance when cutting out the fabric, or mark it on the fabric by hand before cutting out, as shown.

Sometimes it is helpful to have additional markings within the seam allowances when using curved templates or shapes that are difficult to fit, as they will make it easier to join the individual pieces neatly. Cut small notches into the seam allowances where you have made the marks on the template, as shown in the illustration, or draw the marks in pencil.

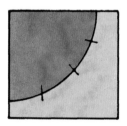 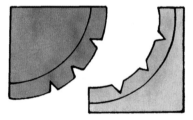

You can buy acrylic patchwork templates, which include a 0.75cm (¼in) seam allowance, in a wide range of designs. Simply run a rotary cutter around the shapes to cut them out. This saves you from having to draw the shape on the fabric and will give you additional design ideas.

Basic appliqué

Appliqué is a simple, effective and enjoyable method of adding decoration to any fabric project. You can use printed motifs or simple coloured shapes cut from contrasting fabrics. Fusible webbing such as Bondaweb or Wonder-Under is used to fix the shapes to the base fabric and to prevent fraying and then usually a tight machine zigzag stitch finishes the edges and provides extra durability.

Free-machine appliqué

With this technique, you simply sew straight stitches over the motifs rather than finishing them with zigzag stitch. This achieves a loose, modern effect, as shown on page 17.

1 Either trace the motifs on to fusible webbing and iron on to the fabric as for the classic method (shown on the opposite page), or iron the webbing on to the appliqué fabric, cut the motifs out freehand and iron on to the background fabric.

2 Place tear-away embroidery stabiliser under the fabric or make a quilt sandwich with wadding and the fabric for the back.

3 Lower the feed dogs on your machine and attach the darning or freehand-quilting foot. Use machine embroidery thread for the top thread and loosen the top tension a little, if required. Sew in a straight line around the outer edges of each motif. A dark thread will reinforce the contrast between the motif and sewn outline, while matching thread will create a softer effect. Overstitching the lines several times will also emphasise the contours.

Wool felt appliqué

Use fusible embroidery stabiliser for this technique. Draw the motifs on the stabiliser and cut out roughly. Fuse the motifs on to the wool felt. Cut out the shapes along the outlines. Fix the felt motifs on the base fabric with a little textile adhesive. Sew around the motifs in running or blanket stitch, if desired. See page 32 for an example of this technique.

Classic machine appliqué

1 Trace the chosen motifs on to fusible webbing and cut out, leaving a generous margin all round, as shown. Remember that the motifs will be reversed (mirror image).

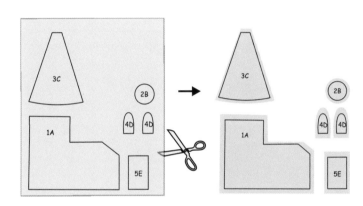

2 Iron the webbing motifs on to the back of the appliqué fabric(s) and leave to cool. Carefully cut out the shapes along the drawn lines, as shown.

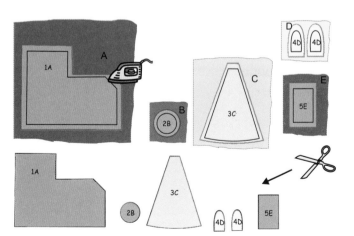

3 Remove the paper backing and iron each motif on to the chosen area of the background fabric. When applying several pieces, take care to fuse them on in order if any shapes overlap, as shown in the illustration.

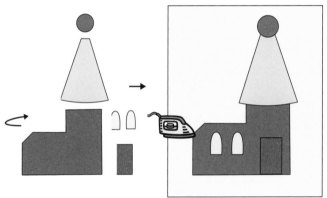

4 Attach an open appliqué foot to your sewing machine and loosen the upper tension a little. Thread the top with matching machine embroidery thread and set your machine for a stitch 0.25–0.3mm long and 3–4mm wide. Ideally test the stitch on some scrap fabric before you begin working on your project.

5 Place stabiliser under the fabric layers, following the manufacturer's instructions, then zigzag stitch around the edges of the motif, as shown. Carefully tear the embroidery stabiliser off when you have finished the appliqué, or remove as instructed by the manufacturer.

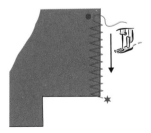

Binding

The easiest way to bind a mug rug is to treat each edge individually, first binding the top and bottom edges and then the sides. For a more professional look, you can mitre the corners using a continuous-binding strip. Most of the projects have 0.75cm (¼in) binding, made from 6.5cm (2½in) wide fabric strips and stitched with a 0.75cm (¼in) seam allowance. If preferred, you can use 0.5cm (³⁄₁₆in) binding using 5.5cm (2¼in) strips and taking a 0.5cm (³⁄₁₆in) seam allowance.

Cut binding

1 Cut two strips the same length as the top and bottom edges. Fold the strips in half lengthways with wrong sides facing and press. With the raw edges facing outwards, pin the strips neatly on the edges of the mug rug and then stitch in place, taking the appropriate seam width.

2 Fold the strips over to the back of the mug rug, covering the stitching line, and pin in place. Cut the two strips for the sides of the mug rug, adding 3cm (1¼in) to the length. Fold these strips in half as before and pin centrally to the corresponding edges of the rug. Fold over the extra 1.5cm (⅝in) at each end. Sew the strips in place

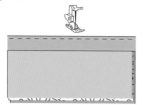

3 Trim the seam allowances slightly at the corners. Fold the two sewn strips over to the back, just covering the stitching and pin or tack in place. Hand stitch all four binding strips to the back or 'stitch in the ditch' (sew along the seam) from the front of the rug.

Continuous binding

This edging is made from a single strip of fabric that is usually 6.5cm (2½in) wide.

1 Press the fabric in half lengthways, right sides out. Working from the middle of one side and with the raw edges facing outwards, pin the binding strip to the front of the rug as far as the first corner. Sew as far as the first corner, omitting the first 10cm (4in) or so of that side. End the seam 0.75cm (¼in) from the edge (corner point) and secure the thread.

2 To sew the next side, rotate the mug rug by 90° and fold the strip up to make a corner at an angle of 45°.

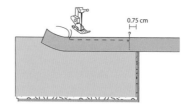
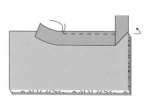

3 Secure this fold by finger pressing – a pin can secure the layers temporarily too. Fold the strip down, level with the top edge of the rug (90° fold), still maintaining the 45° fold you just made. Secure with pins.

4 Sew the strip to the next corner, starting at the 90° fold and secure the seam as before.

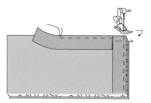

5 Sew the strip to all sides, working each corner in the same way as before. Do not sew the 10cm (4in) of the first seam that you had left unstitched yet. Unfold the binding ends and place one end of the strip over the other. Trim the top strip so that it overlaps the one beneath by 6.5cm (2½in). Fold the ends and sew together at a 45° angle. Press open the seam allowance with your fingers and trim off the excess fabric, leaving a small seam allowance. Refold the binding strip and sew to the rug along the remaining 10cm (4in).

6 Fold the binding over to the back of the mug rug, tucking in the fabric at the corners to a 45° angle. Sew the strip on to the back by hand, covering the previous machine stitching.

Stitches

Some of the designs in this book are hand stitched or include embroidery. Here are the stitches you will need.

Running stitch

Work from right to left (if you are right-handed) by inserting the needle in and out of the fabric at regular intervals. You can work several stitches at once.

Backstitch

Work from right to left. Draw the thread through at A. Insert the needle at B, and pass it out at C. Return to A and then bring the needle out one stitch length beyond C. Continue in this way.

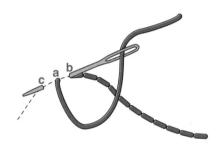

Blanket stitch

This stitch is worked from left to right. Work following the diagrams, making sure that the needle passes over the thread each time and spacing the stitches evenly.

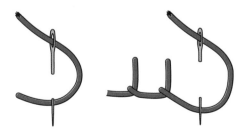

Lazy-daisy stitch

This is made up of chain stitches arranged in a circle and secured by a locking stitch as shown in the diagrams. For small flowers, work from the centre through a single insertion point. For larger flowers, work the stitches around a small circle, as shown in the example.

French knot

The number of times you wrap the thread around the needle determines the size of the knot. Bring the needle out where the knot is to go, then wrap the thread around the needle once or twice, working from the bottom to the top. Insert the needle close to the place it came out.

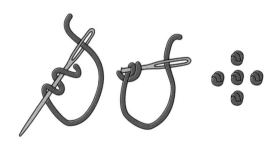

Materials

To make two mug rugs:

- selection of fabric remnants in strong colours (we used red, blue, lilac, pink and patterned)
- 10cm (4in) plain fabric for the binding
- 20cm (8in) complementary fabric for the back
- 20cm (8in) wadding

Cutting out

A seam allowance of 0.75cm (¼in) is included on the binding.

For the patterns, first trace around your template and then add the seam allowance when cutting out (see method).

Square in a Square:

- pattern 1A in patterned fabric
- 4 of pattern 1B in red fabric
- 4 of pattern 1C in blue fabric
- 4 of pattern 1D in patterned fabric

Reveller:

- pattern 2A in patterned fabric
- pattern 2B in lilac fabric
- pattern 2C in pink fabric

Tumbling Triangles:

- 2 of pattern 3A in patterned fabric
- 2 of pattern 3B in blue fabric
- pattern 3B in mirror image in pink fabric
- pattern 3C in lilac fabric

Binding

- 6.5 x 80cm (2½ x 31½in) strip of plain fabric

Geometrics

Trio of mug rugs in geometric shapes by Andreas Wolf

Size: 16 x 16cm (6¼ x 6¼in)   Patterns 1–3 on page 58   **Level of difficulty** ♡ ♡

Method

1 Make templates by copying the patterns on to thin card or template plastic and cut them out (see page 10). For 'Square in a Square' use templates 1A–D; for 'Reveller' use templates 2A–C, and for 'Tumbling Triangles' use templates 3A–C.

2 The three mug rugs are made in the same way. First draw around the templates on the back of the fabrics and cut out the pieces, adding a 0.75cm (¼in) seam allowance.

3 Sew the individual patchwork blocks together, using the illustrations as your guide. Press the seams open.

4 Cut out the wadding and backing fabric a little larger all round than the front piece of patchwork blocks. Pin all three layers together and stitch in the ditch (stitch along the seam lines). Add further quilting to suit the design or fabric pattern, as desired. Trim the wadding and backing fabric to match the size of the front.

5 Fold the binding strip in half lengthways, with wrong sides together, and press it well. With the long cut edges matching the outer edge of the quilt front, sew the binding to the front of the mug rug using either method described on page 12. Turn the edging over to the back and hand stitch into place.

Square in a Square

Reveller

Tumbling Triangles

'Reveller' and 'Tumbling Triangles' are shown in the photograph opposite; 'Square in a Square' is shown on page 2.

Materials

To make two mug rugs:
- ♥ 20cm (8in) white linen
- ♥ green and blue fabric scraps for the flowers and leaves
- ♥ 10cm (4in) green patterned fabric
- ♥ 10cm (4in) blue fabric
- ♥ 10cm (4in) fusible webbing
- ♥ 20cm (8in) fusible wadding
- ♥ matching machine embroidery thread

Cutting out

A seam allowance of 0.75cm (¼in) is included.

- ♥ 19.5 x 13.5cm (7¾ x 5¼in) white linen for the front
- ♥ 23.5 x 17.5cm (9¼ x 7in) white linen for the back
- ♥ 2 strips of green-patterned fabric 3.5 x 13.5cm (1½ x 5¼in) for the side borders
- ♥ 2 strips of green-patterned fabric 3.5 x 29cm (1½ x 11½in) for the top and bottom borders
- ♥ 6.5 x 90cm (2½ x 35½in) strip of blue fabric for the binding, joining 6.5cm (2½in) strips of different fabrics, if desired, for a patchwork finish
- ♥ 23.5 x 17.5cm (9¼ x 7in) wadding

Carpet of Flowers

Mug rug with free-flowing flowers by Renate Bieber

Size: 16 x 22cm (6¼ x 8¾in)   Level of difficulty ♡ ♡

Method

1 Fuse the webbing to the wrong side of the blue and green fabric scraps. Cut out a selection of leaf shapes and some rough circles for the flowers.

2 Arrange the shapes on the white linen and iron into place. You can use our photo for guidance or make your own arrangement.

3 Sew the shorter strips of green patterned fabric on to the sides of the mug rug and then stitch the longer strips to the top and bottom edges to make the border.

4 Iron the wadding on to the back of the appliquéd fabric then pin the back fabric in place, right sides out.

5 Use machine embroidery thread for the top thread on your sewing machine. Free-machine stitch over the flowers, lowering the feed dogs and using a darning or freehand quilting foot. Roughly stitch over the leaf contours for a casual look, allowing your stitches to 'draw' new leaf shapes. Sew along the stems to the middle of the flower circle and then stitch the petals shapes before sewing back down to the base.

6 Trim the mug rug to 22 x 16cm (8¾ x 6¼in), using a patchwork ruler to make sure the corners are square. Attach the binding to the mug rug using the continuous-binding method (see page 12).

Materials

To make two mug rugs:

- 15cm (6in) fabric in white, red and yellow
- 10cm (4in) blue fabric
- 20cm (8in) fabric for the back
- 20cm (8in) wadding
- 2m (2¼yd) black bias binding
- black mercerised thread

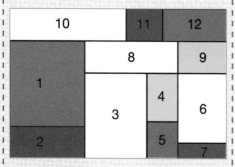

Mug Rug 1

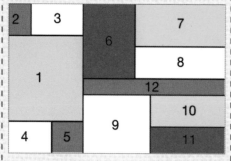

Mug Rug 2

Use black thread for joining the fabric pieces so you do not have to change colour when zigzagging over the mercerised thread.

Prime Time

Mondrian-style mug rug by Susanne Rosensträter

Size: 22.5 x 14.5cm (9 x 5¾in)   Level of difficulty ♡

Cutting out

A seam allowance of 0.75cm (¼in) is included.

- 24 x 16cm (9½ x 6¼in) fabric for the back of each mug rug
- 24 x 16cm (9½ x 6¼in) wadding for each mug rug

Mug rug 1:

- red fabric: 9.5 x 9.5cm (3¾ x 3¾in) for part 1; 4.5 x 5cm (1¾ x 2in) for part 5; 8 x 4.5cm (1⅛ x 1¾in) for part 12
- white fabric: 6.5 x 9.5cm (2½ x 3¾in) for part 3; 6.5 x 8cm (2½ x 3⅛in) for part 6; 9.5 x 4.5cm (3¾ x 1¾in) for part 8; 12.5 x 4.5cm (5 x 1¾in) for part 10
- yellow fabric: 4.5 x 6cm (1¾ x 2³⁄₈in) for part 4; 6.5 x 4.5cm (2½ x 1¾in) for part 9
- blue fabric: 9.5 x 4.5cm (3¾ x 1¾in) for part 2; 6.5 x 3cm (2½ x 1¼in) for part 7; 5 x 4.5cm (2 x 1¾in) for part 11

Mug rug 2:

- yellow fabric: 9.5 x 9.5cm (3¾ x 3¾in) for part 1; 10.5 x 5.5cm (4⅛ x 2¼in) for part 7; 9 x 3.5cm (3½ x 1³⁄₈in) for part 10
- red fabric: 4.5 x 4.5cm (1¾ x 1¾in) for part 2; 4.5 x 4.5cm (1¾ x 1¾in) for part 5; 14.5 x 3cm (5¾ x 1¼in) for part 12
- white fabric: 6.5 x 4.5cm (2½ x 1¾in) for part 3; 6.5 x 4.5cm (2½ x 1¾in) for part 4; 10.5 x 4.5cm (4⅛ x 1¾in) for part 8; 7 x 7cm (2¾ x 2¾in) for part 9
- blue fabric: 5.5 x 8.5cm (5¼ x 3¼in) for part 6; 9 x 4.5cm (3½ x 1¾in) for part 11

Method

1 Referring to the appropriate diagram, sew two adjacent pieces of the mug rug right sides together, such as pieces 1 and 2 on rug 1. Press the seam open. Turn the fabric right side up and lay mercerised thread over the seam just sewn. Set your machine length and width to 1.5 and zigzag over the thread. Trim the thread. Join and finish all the pieces of your mug rug in this way.

2 Pin the patchwork front, wadding and back together, right sides out. If you like, you can quilt a few squares using black thread. Trim the wadding and back to the same size as the front.

3 Attach the binding to the mug rug using the continuous-binding method (page 12).

Materials

For two mug rugs:
- ♥ 25cm (10in) white fabric
- ♥ scraps of patterned fabrics
- ♥ scrap of fabric with printed motif
- ♥ 20cm (8in) fusible webbing
- ♥ 20cm (8in) thin wadding
- ♥ white or coordinating thread

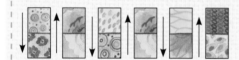

Figure 1

Figure 2

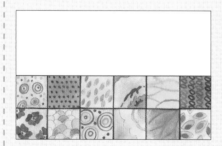

Figure 3

Samplers with Style

Mug rugs to try out new skills by Veronika Mickenhagen-Cox

Size: 24 x 20cm (9½ x 8in)   **Level of difficulty** ♡ ♡

Cutting out

A seam allowance of 0.5cm (³⁄₁₆in) is included.

For each mug rug:
- ♥ 12 pieces of patterned fabric 6.5 x 6.5cm (2½ x 2½in)
- ♥ 32 x 12cm (12½ x 4¾in) white fabric for the front
- ♥ 34 x 24cm (13½ x 9½in) white fabric for the back
- ♥ 34 x 24cm (13½ x 9½in) wadding

Method

1 Make both mug rugs in the same way. Stitch the squares together in pairs and press the seam allowances to one side. Lay out the pairs so the seam allowances go in opposite directions (figure 1). Join the pairs into blocks of four (figure 2). Join the blocks and then join the white strip to the top edge (figure 3).

2 Iron the webbing on to the back of your motif fabric and cut out the motif exactly. Arrange the motif on your pieced fabric and iron into place. Trim the entire thing into a pleasing shape.

3 Pin the pieced fabric on to the wadding. Stitch around the appliqué motif in a matching thread, lowering the feed dogs and using the darning or freehand-quilting foot. Stitch close to the outer edges of the motif and highlight details as desired. Quilt the white top area of the fabric in a pleasing design.

4 Trim the wadding to the size of the front. Put the front and back right sides together and sew around the outside, leaving an opening at the bottom so you can turn out the mug rug. Trim the back to the size of the front. Make a few cuts in the corners of the seam allowances just up to the seam. Turn the mug rug right side out, tuck in the seam allowance at the opening and topstitch around the edge.

A Treat for the Eyes

Muffin-shaped mug rug by Peggy Donda-Kobert

Size: 17 x 20cm (6¾ x 8in)   Pattern 4 on page 60   **Level of difficulty** ♡ ♡

Materials

To make two mug rugs:
- 15cm (6in) brown fabric
- 10cm (4in) patterned pink or lilac fabric
- fabric scraps in red or lilac
- 20cm (8in) fusible wadding
- 15cm (6in) firm fusible embroidery stabiliser
- scraps of fusible webbing
- brown thread
- machine embroidery thread in pink or white

Cutting out

No seam allowances are included.

- Use the patterns on page 60 to make templates for the icing and base of the muffins. For each mug rug, trace two icing sections on to the back of the patterned pink or lilac fabric, one in a mirror image, and trace two base pieces on to the back of the brown fabric.
- Cut out one base and icing from wadding, as well as one icing in stabiliser. Cut out all the pieces, adding a seam allowance all round.

Method

1 Make both mug rugs in the same way. Iron the corresponding wadding on to the back of one base and one icing, and iron the stabiliser on to the back of the other icing. Place the base pieces right side together and sew along the sides and bottom edge. Turn the base out and topstitch close to the edge in matching thread. Topstitch three evenly spaced lines down the length of the muffin (see the photograph for guidance).

2 Pin the icing pieces together, right sides out, and insert the muffin base between the layers. Set the stitch width on your machine to 0.3–0.4, and adjust the top tension, if necessary. Work close zigzag all round the icing, using machine embroidery thread for both the top and bobbin threads and making sure that the needle just passes over the very edge of the icing fabric.

3 Transfer the strawberry or heart pattern to the fusible webbing and cut out, leaving a generous margin all round. Iron on to the back of the lilac or red fabric scrap, and cut out carefully along the drawn lines. Fuse to a second scrap of fabric and trim off the excess. Sew around the outside either using zigzag stitch on the machine or by hand in blanket stitch (see page 13). Sew on to the muffin with tiny hand stitches.

Materials

To make two mug rugs:
- ♥ 20cm (8in) lilac fabric for the front and back
- ♥ assorted coloured fabric scraps
- ♥ 15cm (6in) bright striped fabric for the binding
- ♥ 20cm (8in) fusible webbing
- ♥ 20cm (8in) wadding
- ♥ black machine embroidery thread
- ♥ black embroidery cotton
- ♥ water-soluble marker pen

Cutting out

A seam allowance of 0.75cm (¼in) is included.

For each mug rug:
- ♥ 2 pieces of lilac checked fabric 16 x 23cm (6¼ x 9in) for the front and back
- ♥ 2 pieces of bright striped fabric 16 x 6.5cm (6¼ x 2½in) for binding the top and bottom
- ♥ 2 pieces of bright striped fabric 25 x 6.5cm (10 x 2½in) for binding the sides
- ♥ 16 x 23cm (6¼ x 9in) wadding

You can use free-machine stitch to stitch around the appliqué pieces. Lower the feed dogs and use the darning or freehand quilting foot. Stitch close to the outer edges of the motifs.

Monkeying Around

Mug rugs with monkeys by Beate Pöhlmann

Size: 16 x 23cm (6¼ x 9in)   **Patterns 5 and 6 on page 59**   **Level of difficulty** ♡

Method

1 Transfer the monkey patterns (the outlines of the body with arms, legs and tail, the head, tummy, muzzle, ears, branch and leaves) on to the fusible webbing. Cut out, leaving a generous allowance all round and iron on to the back of your chosen fabrics. Cut out the motifs exactly. Arrange the individual elements as shown in the photograph, overlapping where required as shown on the pattern pieces. Iron all the pieces into place.

2 Set the machine to a stitch length of 1–1.5 and stitch around each piece using black thread. Draw on the face using a water-soluble fabric marker and then hand sew in black thread using backstitch with satin stitch for the nostrils.

3 Press the appliqué and place on the wadding and back piece, right sides out. Pin and then stitch the three layers together and zigzag neatly around the edges.

4 Fold the binding strips in half lengthways, right sides out, and press. Stitch the shorter strips to the top and bottom of the back, flush with the edge, and then sew the longer strips to the left and right. Fold the strips over on to the front and topstitch into place (see page 12).

It's All in the Name

Named mug rugs by Peggy Donda-Kobert

Size: 21 x 15cm (8¼ x 6in) **Level of difficulty** ♡

Materials

To make two mug rugs:

- ♥ 20cm (8in) linen
- ♥ various fabric scraps for the letters and binding
- ♥ 10cm (4in) fusible webbing
- ♥ 20cm (8in) tear-away embroidery stabiliser
- ♥ 20cm (8in) fusible wadding
- ♥ matching machine embroidery thread
- ♥ bias-binding maker (optional)

Cutting out

A seam allowance of 0.75cm (¼in) is included.

For each mug rug:

- ♥ 2 pieces of linen 15 x 21cm (6 x 8¼in) for the front and back
- ♥ 15 x 21cm (6 x 8¼in) wadding

If you do not have a binding maker, press the binding strip in half lengthways, wrong sides together. Unfold and then press each long edge in to meet the centre fold line, wrong sides together. Press again. Fold in half lengthways again so you have four layers and press.

Method

1 Type the letters for each name on your computer in a suitable typeface – Arial Black and Impact are ideal and installed on almost every computer – and enlarge to about 200pt. Print out the letters and transfer a mirror image of each one on to the fusible webbing so that the letter is the right way round when appliquéd. (Turn the paper over and hold it up to the window or work on a light box to do this.) Cut out each letter, leaving a generous margin all round. Iron the letters on to the back of your chosen fabric scraps and then cut out the motifs exactly. Arrange on the front linen rectangle and iron on.

2 Fix embroidery stabiliser to the back of the appliquéd linen. Thread the sewing machine with thread to match the letters and attach an appliqué foot – because the appliqué foot has a wide opening, you can easily see when you need to turn the work or when you have got to the corner of a letter.

3 Set the stitch length to 0.25–0.5 and loosen the top tension so that the lower thread does not show on the surface. Zigzag all round each letter, making sure that the needle goes over the edge. Tear the embroidery stabiliser off the back.

4 Iron the wadding on to the back of the front piece and pin the front to the back, right sides out. Sew the three layers together on all sides, working close to the edge.

5 Binding: cut fabric scraps into 4cm (1½in) wide strips of varying lengths. Join the strips to make a single length about 90cm (35½in) long, and iron into shape using a bias-binding maker (or see the tip). Sew the binding to the front edge of the mug rug, along the first fold line of the binding, fold over to the back (centre fold matches the fabric edge) and attach with small hand stitches so that the final fold of the binding just covers the previous stitching. (See also continuous binding, page 12).

Materials

- 20cm (8in) green fabric
- 15cm (6in) rose-patterned fabric
- 10cm (4in) bright pink fabric
- 10cm (4in) fusible webbing
- 20cm (8in) fusible tear-away embroidery stabiliser
- 20cm (8in) wadding
- matching thread or embroidery cotton

Cutting out

A seam allowance of 0.75cm (¼in) is included.

- 2 pieces of green fabric 26 x 15.5cm (10¼ x 6⅛in) for the front and back
- 26 x 15.5cm (10¼ x 6⅛in) wadding
- 6 pieces of rose fabric 6 x 6cm (2⅜ x 2⅜in)
- 6 pieces wadding 6 x 6cm (2⅜ x 2⅜in)

Tea for One

Mug rug with teacup and pot by Beate Mazek

Size: 29 x 14cm (11½ x 5½in)   Pattern 7 on page 60   Level of difficulty ♡

Method

1 Trace the pattern pieces for the teapot and cup (body of the pot, handle, spout, lid, cup, handle and saucer) on the fusible webbing and cut, adding a generous margin all round. Iron the cup and pot on to the back of the rose fabric, and the two handles, spout, lid and saucer on to the pink fabric. Cut out the motifs exactly. Arrange the shapes on the front rectangle, overlapping them as indicated on the pattern pieces, and iron into place.

2 Place the tear-away embroidery stabiliser under the fabric and work blanket stitch all around each piece in matching thread or embroidery cotton. Carefully tear the embroidery stabiliser off the back.

3 Copy the semicircle pattern six times on to the back of the rose-patterned fabric (not the rose-patterned squares). Cut out, adding a seam allowance all round. Place one semicircle on a rose-patterned square, right sides together, and then pin these to a wadding square. Sew together around the semicircle, leaving the straight edge unstitched for turning. Trim the excess fabric and wadding, leaving a small seam allowance on the fabric but trimming the wadding back as far as possible. Turn the semicircle right sides out and press. Repeat with the other five semicircles.

4 Tack three half-circles along each side of the appliquéd rectangle with raw edges matching. Pin the back piece right sides down on top and the wadding underneath. Sew all round, leaving a gap in one long edge to turn through. Trim the seam allowance at the corners. Turn out the mug rug, tuck in the seam allowances at the opening and slipstitch it closed.

Materials

- 15cm (6in) light brown fabric
- 10cm (4in) fabric in a geometric pattern
- 35cm (14in) coordinating patterned fabric
- 25cm (10in) wadding

Figure 1

Figure 2

Figure 3

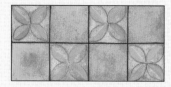

Figure 4

Pocket Rug

Mug rug with pocket and mug cosy by Kerstin Porsch

Size: 28.5 x 19.5cm (11¼ x 7¾in)　**Level of difficulty** ♡

Cutting out

A seam allowance of 0.75cm (¼in) is included.

- 5 x 60cm (2 x 23½in) light brown fabric for the checkerboard pattern
- 5 x 60cm (2 x 23½in) geometric fabric for the checkerboard pattern
- 10 x 19cm (4 x 7½in) light brown fabric for spoon pocket background
- 10 x 20cm (4 x 8in) light brown fabric for spoon pocket
- 3 pieces coordinating patterned fabric 4 x 19cm (1½ x 7½in)
- 2 pieces turquoise and brown fabric for the top and bottom edging 4 x 30cm (1½ x 12in)
- 30 x 21cm (12 x 8¼in) coordinating patterned fabric for the back
- 30 x 21cm (12 x 8¼in) wadding

Method

1 Join the two 5cm (2in) strips for the checkerboard pattern along one long edge (figure 1). Press the seam open. Cut this strip into ten sections 5cm (2in) wide (figure 2). Sew two sections together to make a row (figure 3). Sew a total of five rows. Join the rows together, rotating alternate rows by 180 degrees (figure 4).

2 Attach a 4 x 19cm (1½ x 7½in) strip of coordinating fabric to the left and right sides of the chequerboard.

3 Fold the pocket fabric in half widthways with wrong sides facing. Tack the folded pocket to the pocket background, matching three edges but not the folded top edge. Sew the pocket to the strip on the right of the chequerboard and then attach the remaining 4 x 19cm (1½ x 7½in) strip to the other side of the pocket.

4 Attach the two edging strips to the top and bottom edges. Place the front on the back piece, right sides together, and then pin the wadding on top. Stitch together all round, leaving a small gap along one long edge for turning. Trim the seam allowances at the corners and turn right sides out. Tuck in the seam allowances at the opening and close with small hand stitches. Stitch in the ditch (sew along the seam lines).

Mug cosy

♥ Measure the height and circumference of the mug. Cut a rectangle to this dimension from the light brown fabric, patterned fabric and wadding.

♥ You will also need 2 tie strips, 5 x 50cm (2 x 19¾in)

Pin the two fabric rectangles right sides together with the wadding on top and stitch all round, leaving a gap for turning. Turn out, trim and finish as for the mug rug. Fold each tie strip in half lengthways, right sides together, sew the long sides together and turn out. Pin centrally on the rectangle with one above and one below the mug handle. Topstitch in place along the long edges. Knot the ends.

Materials

- 30cm (12in) dotty cream fabric
- fabric scrap with large flowers
- wool felt scraps in yellow, turquoise, green, red-brown and dark brown
- 10cm (4in) fusible webbing
- 20cm (8in) wadding
- yellow embroidery cotton

Figure 1

Figure 2

Flower Power

Retro mug rug by Regine Joskowiak

Size: 23 x 17cm (9 x 6¾in)   Pattern 8 on page 59   Level of difficulty ♡

Cutting out

A seam allowance of 0.75cm (¼in) is included.

- 11 x 11cm (4¼ x 4¼in) flower fabric
- 4.5 x 14cm (1¾ x 5½in) yellow felt
- 4.5 x 14cm (1¾ x 5½in) turquoise felt
- 4.5 x 14cm (1¾ x 5½in) green felt
- 4.5 x 14cm (1¾ x 5½in) red-brown felt
- 8 x 17cm (3⅛ x 6¾in) dark brown felt
- 25 x 19cm (10 x 7½in) dotty fabric for the back
- 25 x 19cm (10 x 7½in) wadding
- 6.5 x 95cm (2½ x 37½in) dotty fabric for binding

Method

1 Place the red-brown felt strip on the 11cm (4¼in) floral square, right sides together, and sew up to approximately half the length of the square (figure 1). Press the seam open. Sew on the green felt strip in its entirety (figure 2), then the turquoise and yellow strips. Finally, stitch the first seam to the end. Sew the dark brown rectangle to the left-hand side.

2 Transfer the patterns for the two petal sections and flower centre on to the fusible webbing and cut out, leaving a generous margin all round. Iron the pieces on to the appropriate felt scraps and then cut out the motifs exactly.

3 Sew tiny French knots (see page 13) on the flower centre using two strands of embroidery cotton, and then embroider the veining with straight stitches on the red-brown petals. Fuse the flower in position on the mug rug.

4 Pin the front, wadding and back together, right sides out. Stitch in the ditch (stitch along the seam lines). Attach the binding strip to the edges using the continuous-binding method (see page 12).

The felt flower on this mug rug echoes the design on the floral fabric. If you have a bold flower shape on your fabric too, trace the fabric motif to use as a template for your felt flower.

Materials

- 10cm (4in) turquoise patterned fabric for the binding
- scraps in beige and dark beige
- wool felt scraps in white, pink and pale pink
- 20cm (8in) thin wadding
- 20cm (8in) fusible embroidery stabiliser
- cotton thread in pink, dusky pink and dark brown
- water-soluble marker pen
- textile adhesive

Cutting out

A seam allowance of 0.5cm (³/₁₆in) is included.

- 30 x 25cm (12 x 10in) dotty turquoise fabric for the front
- 22 x 16cm (8¾ x 6¼in) dotty turquoise fabric for the back
- 2 strips patterned turquoise fabric 22 x 5.5cm (8¾ x 2¼in) for the top and bottom binding
- 2 strips patterned turquoise fabric 20 x 5.5cm (8 x 2¼in) for the side binding
- 22 x 16cm (8¾ x 6¼in) wadding

Sew Time

Mug rug with sewing machine by Christa Rolf

Size: 22 x 16cm (8¾ x 6¼in)   Pattern 9 on page 61   **Level of difficulty** ♡ ♡

Method

1 Mark an area 21 x 15cm (8¼ x 6in) centred on the right side of the front fabric (so that you put the appliqué and embroidery in the correct positions). The broken line on the pattern shows the area that will later be seen.

2 Enlarge the patterns to full size and then transfer the sewing machine and its stand to the uncoated side of the embroidery stabiliser. Cut out and iron on to the right side of your chosen fabric. Cut out the individual motifs, adding a seam allowance of about 0.5cm (³/₁₆in) all round. Hand stitch the pieces in place, pushing the seam allowance under with your needle as you go (or press it to the back first). Pull off the embroidery backing and remove any tacking threads.

3 Transfer the two patterns for the cotton reel and the little flower on to the embroidery stabiliser and cut out roughly. Iron the cotton reel on to white felt and the flower on to pale pink felt and then cut out. Pull off the embroidery stabiliser and stick both motifs in place using textile adhesive.

4 Backstitch the outlines of the hand wheel, spool holder and needle in brown thread, then backstitch the thread in dusky pink. Sew a French knot in the centre of the flower and two single chain stitches in dusky pink next to the flower.

5 Embroider the pink wool strip before cutting it to shape. First draw the words on the wool felt, then work the letters in brown backstitches. Stitch the heart shape in dusky pink. Cut the embroidered wool felt to shape so that it can be caught in the binding at the bottom. Stick it on with textile adhesive and work running stitches around the edges. Cut out the hearts, stick them on with textile adhesive and then work blanket stitch around the edges.

6 Trim the front to 22 x 16cm (8¾ x 6¼in). Tack the front, wadding and back together, right sides out. Attach the binding following the instructions on page 12, attaching the strips to the top and bottom edges first and then to the sides.

Materials

- ♥ 20cm (8in) red fabric
- ♥ 20cm (8in) pink checked fabric
- ♥ various fabric scraps in green, pink and beige including one with a large rose pattern and one with a small rose pattern
- ♥ 10cm (4in) fusible webbing
- ♥ 20cm (8in) fusible wadding
- ♥ red and beige embroidery cotton
- ♥ water-soluble marker pen

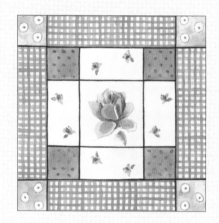

Pretty in Pink

Mug rug with a cup and rose by Sabine Günther

Size: 24 x 16.5cm (9½ x 6½in)   Pattern 10 on page 61   **Level of difficulty** ♡ ♡

Cutting out

A seam allowance of 0.75cm (¼in) is included.

Patchwork block:
- ♥ 6.5 x 6.5cm (2½ x 2½in) large-rose patterned fabric
- ♥ 4 squares of red fabric 4 x 4cm (1½ x 1½in)
- ♥ 4 pieces of small-patterned rose fabric 4 x 6.5cm (1½ x 2½in)
- ♥ 4 squares of green fabric 4 x 4cm (1½ x 1½in)
- ♥ 4 pieces of pink checked fabric 4 x 11.5cm (1½ x 4½in)

Appliqué block:
- ♥ 9 x 9.5cm (3½ x 3¾in) pale fabric for the top block
- ♥ 9 x 6cm (3½ x 2⅜in) beige fabric for the centre block
- ♥ 9 x 4cm (3½ x 1½in) small-rose patterned fabric for the bottom block

Back and edging:
- ♥ 26 x 19cm (10¼ x 7½in) pink checked fabric for the back
- ♥ 26 x 19cm (10¼ x 7½in) wadding
- ♥ 6.5 x 92cm (2½ x 36¼in) red fabric for the binding

Method

1 Sew the sections for the patchwork block together following the diagram on the left. If you wish, you can embroider a name in backstitch using red thread, as shown in the photograph. Join the three background sections for the appliqué block together then join the appliqué block to the patchwork block.

2 Trace the teacup, handle and saucer patterns on to fusible webbing. Cut out, leaving a generous margin all round. Iron the cup and handle on to the back of some pink fabric and the saucer on to the back of the red fabric. Cut out the shapes exactly. Arrange the cup and saucer on the appliqué block, placing the cup over the saucer as indicated on the pattern, and iron in place. Work blanket stitch around each piece (see page 13). Draw the steam in water-soluble marker pen as shown on the pattern and stitch over the lines in beige backstitch.

3 Pin the finished front to the back fabric with the wadding in between, right sides out, and quilt by hand or machine. Cut the wadding and backing to match the front and bind the edges with the red fabric strip, following the instructions for continuous binding on page 12.

Baker's Shop

Baker's shop mug rug by Heike Ziefuss

Size: 25 x 18cm (10 x 7in)   **Pattern 11 on page 61**   **Level of difficulty** ♡ ♡

Materials

For two mug rugs:

- ♥ fabric: 25cm (10in) patterned beige, 10cm (4in) patterned red, 15cm (6in) pale beige and a remnant with small cake motifs
- ♥ wool felt scraps: light green, red, pale yellow and brown
- ♥ 25cm (10in) fusible wadding
- ♥ 15cm (6in) fusible webbing
- ♥ 15cm (6in) embroidery stabiliser
- ♥ 30cm (12in) white lace 2.5cm (1in) wide
- ♥ quilting thread in light green and off-white
- ♥ cotton thread in mid-brown
- ♥ small heart-shaped buttons
- ♥ water-soluble marker pen
- ♥ pinking shears

Cutting out

Fabric:

- ♥ 28 x 16cm (11 x 6¼in) patterned beige for the house
- ♥ 26.5 x 21cm (10½ x 8¼in) patterned beige for the back
- ♥ 10 x 15cm (4 x 6in) pale beige for the doorway (behind the door)
- ♥ 11 x 5cm (4¼ x 2in) pale beige for the display window
- ♥ 8.5 x 26.5cm (3⅜ x 10½in) patterned red for the roof

Wool felt:

- ♥ 11 x 1.5cm (4¼ x ⅝in) red for the awning
- ♥ 5.5 x 8cm (2¼ x 3⅛in) green for the door
- ♥ 4.5 x 3cm (1¾ x 1¼in) pale yellow for the door window
- ♥ 3 x 9.5cm (1¼ x 3¾in) brown for the chimney
- ♥ 2 of each of the skylight pattern in pale yellow

Method

1 Trace the pattern for the baker on to the doorway rectangle and then sew along the lines using small backstitches in mid-brown. Trim the fabric to 5.5 x 8cm (2¼ x 3⅛in) and then fuse webbing on to the back.

2 Cut two cake motifs, roughly 4 x 5cm (1½ x 2in) and iron fusible webbing on to the backs. Cut out the cakes, adding a tiny (1mm) allowance all round. Fuse in place on the display window and then stitch all round each one in tight zigzag, using stabiliser underneath. Carefully tear off the stabiliser and iron fusible webbing to the back of the display window.

3 Iron the display window and doorway on to the house and zigzag the edges in light green thread.

4 Trim the lower edge of the red awning with pinking shears and then sew the top edge to the display window. Fix the felt door window to the door using spray adhesive and sew all round in blanket stitch. Indicate the glazing bars of the window with running stitch. Sew the right side of the door to the right side of the doorway using blanket stitch. Trim the house to 26.5 x 14.5cm (10½ x 5¾in).

5 Secure the two skylights to the roof with fusible webbing and then stitch with blanket stitch and running stitch as before. Trim the sides of the roof on a slant. Tack the lace to the top of the house and then sew the house to the roof with right sides facing.

6 Cut wadding to fit the house and iron it on to the wrong side of the fabric. Trim the back of the mug rug to the same size as the front. Fold the chimney strip in half widthways and tack to the roof. Pin the front and back pieces right sides together and sew all round, leaving a gap in the bottom edge for turning and catching the chimney in the seam. Turn out the house and sew up the opening. Topstitch all round then sew on the buttons.

Materials

For two mug rugs:
- ♥ 20cm (8in) plain green fabric
- ♥ scraps of plain fabric in red, yellow, royal blue and dark blue
- ♥ 10cm (4in) coordinating patterned fabrics in blue and green
- ♥ 15cm (6in) fusible webbing
- ♥ 20cm (8in) tear-away embroidery stabiliser
- ♥ 20cm (8in) wadding
- ♥ matching embroidery threads
- ♥ quilting thread (optional)

Cutting out

A seam allowance of 0.75cm (¼in) is included.

Each mug rug:
- ♥ 26 x 19cm (10¼ x 7½in) green fabric for the back
- ♥ 26 x 19cm (10¼ x 7½in) wadding

Mug rug with flower:
- ♥ 7 strips of green/blue patterned fabric 26 x 4cm (10¼ x 1½in) for the front
- ♥ 6.5 x 92cm (2½ x 36¼in) blue patterned fabric for binding

Mug rug with houses:
- ♥ 26 x 19cm (10¼ x 7½in) green fabric for the front
- ♥ 6.5 x 92cm (2½ x 36¼in) light green patterned fabric for binding

Two's Company

Mug rug duo by Ulla Stewart

Size: 24 x 16cm (9½ x 6¼in)   Patterns 12 and 13 on page 62   **Level of difficulty** ♡

Method

Flower mug rug:

1 Sew the seven fabric strips together lengthways. Transfer the patterns for the flower and flower centre (see page 62) to the fusible webbing and cut out, leaving a generous margin all round. Iron the flower on to the back of the red fabric and the centre on to the back of the yellow fabric. Cut around the motifs exactly. Now position them on the pieced rectangle and fuse in place.

2 Place embroidery stabiliser under the fabric and zigzag or embroider around the edges of the appliqué pieces in matching thread. Carefully tear off the embroidery stabiliser.

3 Pin the appliquéd front, wadding and back together, right sides out. Stitch in the ditch (quilt along the seam lines) of the pieced section.

4 Trim the mug rug to 24 x 16cm (9½ x 6¼in), making sure that the corners are square, and then bind the edges using the continuous-binding method (see page 12).

Houses mug rug:

1 Transfer the patterns for the parts of the houses (houses, roofs, windows and doors) to the fusible webbing and cut out, leaving a generous margin. Draw the path freehand, roughly 26cm (10¼in) long (see the photograph) and transfer to webbing. Fuse the pieces to the back of the appropriate fabrics and then cut out exactly. Position them on the front rectangle, overlapping pieces as shown on the pattern, and fuse in place. Place embroidery stabiliser under the fabric and zigzag or embroider around the edges of the appliqué pieces in matching thread. Work long stitches over the windows to indicate the glazing bars or mark these on with a permanent fabric marker. Carefully tear off the embroidery stabiliser.

2 Pin the appliquéd front, wadding and back together, and continue as for the flower mug rug but without quilting the layers.

Materials

- 88 hexagons, 12mm (½in) across, cut from freezer paper or lightweight copy paper (acrylic template available from patchwork suppliers)
- 25cm (10in) raspberry-coloured fabric
- 10cm (4in) each of pink, cream, beige, dark beige, beige patterned and beige striped fabric
- 20cm (8in) wadding
- light brown embroidery cotton
- water-soluble marker pen

Cutting out

Cut strips 3cm (1¼in) wide from the fabrics for the hexagons. If using freezer paper, iron each hexagon on to the wrong side of the fabric and cut around the hexagon, adding about 0.75cm (¼in) all round for seam allowances. If using A4 paper, pin or tack the paper in place before cutting the fabric, again adding a seam allowance all round.

Hexagons:
- 6 in pink fabric
- 6 in cream fabric
- 6 in dark beige fabric
- 6 in beige patterned fabric
- 12 in beige striped fabric
- 34 in beige fabric (background)
- 18 in raspberry-coloured fabric (flower centres and edge)

Hand-stitched Hexagons

English patchwork mug rug by Regine Joskowiak

Size: 25 x 15cm (10 x 6in)   **Level of difficulty** ♡ ♡

Method

1 Carefully fold the surplus fabric around the back of each paper hexagon and tack in place. Be as precise as possible.

2 Stitch the hexagons together as follows. Place two hexagons directly on top of one another, right sides together, and oversew one matching edge together, being careful not to stitch through the paper. Open out the hexagons, lay on the next hexagon and stitch as before. Repeat until all the hexagons are joined. Remove the tacking, pull out the paper and trim the edges of the mug rug to the finished shape.

3 Cut the raspberry-coloured fabric and wadding to the size of the front. Place the front and back right sides together, then place both on the wadding and pin through all layers. Sew together all round, leaving an opening at the bottom for turning. Trim the wadding tight to the seam, and trim the fabric seam allowances at the angles. Turn the mug rug out and close the opening by hand. Topstitch all round, close to the edge. Hand quilt the flower centres.

Join the hexagons for each flower first and then join the flowers using the background hexagons – any little adjustments will be less obvious if they are made on the background areas than on the flowers.

Cathedral Windows

Atarashii-style mug rug by Verena Surerus

Size: 28 x 16cm (11 x 6¼in)   Template 15 on page 63   **Level of difficulty** ♡ ♡

Materials

- ♥ 15cm (6in) grey checked fabric
- ♥ 20cm (8in) grey patterned fabric
- ♥ 20cm (8in) thin wadding
- ♥ 80cm (31½in) grey patterned bias binding
- ♥ grey machine embroidery thread

Cutting out

The following measurements include a 0.75cm (¼in) seam allowance.

Make the three templates (A, B and C) using the patterns on page 63. Mark the outer and inner sides on piece A. Trace the templates on to the backs of the relevant fabrics and cut out, adding a 0.5cm (³⁄₁₆in) seam allowance all round each piece.

Now cut the following:

- ♥ 6 of A in grey checked fabric
- ♥ 2 of B in grey patterned fabric
- ♥ 1 of C in grey checked fabric
- ♥ 20 x 30cm (8 x 12in) grey patterned fabric for the back
- ♥ 20 x 30cm (8 x 12in) wadding

Make your own bias binding from fabric using a bias-binding maker (see page 26).

Method

1 Working by hand, sew piece C between the two B sections, taking a 0.5cm (³⁄₁₆in) seam allowance. Sew the inner side of the six A pieces to the remaining sides of the B sections. Press the seams open carefully.

2 Pin the front, wadding and back together, right sides out. Machine embroider all round each B section. Use machine embroidery thread for the top thread on your machine and loosen the top tension a little, if necessary. Trim the wadding and back fabric to the size of the front.

3 Attach the bias binding from the front (see page 26). Allow a little extra width in the outer curves so that it sits well when turned to the back and pull it a little tighter in the inner curves so that it is not too loose here. Fold the binding over to the back and stitch down with small hand stitches.

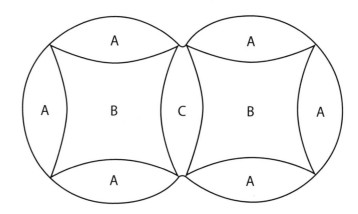

Materials

- 20cm (8in) white cotton or linen fabric
- red-and-white fabric scraps with patterns and stripes
- 20cm (8in) fusible wadding
- 20cm (8in) tear-away embroidery stabiliser
- 50cm (20in) red rickrack braid
- 20cm (8in) white crocheted lace
- red machine embroidery thread
- white embroidery cotton
- water-soluble marker pen

Cutting out

A seam allowance of 0.75cm (¼in) is included.

- 16 x 10.5cm (6¼ x 4⅛in) white cotton/linen for the front
- 22.5 x 16.5cm (9 x 6½in) white cotton/linen for the back
- 2 pieces of patterned fabric 4.5 x 10.5cm (1¾ x 4⅛in) for the side borders
- 6.5 x 90cm (2½ x 35½in) striped fabric for binding
- 22.5 x 16.5cm (9 x 6½in) wadding

Good Morning

Red-and-white breakfast mug rug by Renate Bieber

Size: 22 x 16cm (8¾ x 6¼in)   **Level of difficulty** ♡ ♡

Method

1 Attach the side border strips to the white fabric, with right sides facing, and sew the white crochet lace on the seams just sewn, as shown in the photograph. Tack the rickrack braid about 0.5cm (⅜in) from the top and bottom edges. Join 4.5cm (1¾in) strips of patterned fabric in different lengths and trim to make two pieces 4.5 x 22cm (1¾ x 8¾in). Sew the strips to the top and bottom of the front.

2 Iron the wadding on to the back rectangle and pin to the front, right sides out. Embroider in white blanket stitch on the pieced strips adjacent to the braid.

3 Trim the mug rug to 22 x 16cm (8¾ x 6¼in) and edge with the striped binding using the continuous-binding method (see page 12).

If you wish, embroider a greeting such as 'Good Morning' across the middle of the rug mug. This should be done before step 1. Choose a computer font you like for the wording, print the words out with a font size of about 100pt and then transfer the letters to the white fabric using a water-soluble marker pen. Lower the machine feed dogs and fit a darning or freehand quilting foot to your machine. Place the embroidery stabiliser underneath the letters and sew around them using a small zigzag stitch (width about 1.5) and machine embroidery thread. Wipe off the marker pen using a damp cloth and leave to dry. Tear off the embroidery stabiliser.

Materials

♥ 20cm (8in) beige coffee-themed fabric
♥ 10cm (4in) brown patterned fabric
♥ scrap of brown striped fabric
♥ 20cm (8in) wadding
♥ brown machine-quilting thread
♥ water-soluble marker pen

Preparation

Enlarge the pattern on page 61 to size and use it to make templates for the handle, cup and saucer (see page 10).

A small seam allowance of 0.5cm (³/₁₆in) is best for motifs with tight curves because the seams lie flatter. Alternatively, use a larger seam allowance and then trim it back before turning out.

Coffee Time

Cup-shaped mug rug by Christa Rolf

Size: 23 x 14cm (9 x 5½in)   Pattern 16 on page 61   **Level of difficulty** ♡ ♡

Method

1 Enlarge the pattern pieces to full size. Referring to the photograph, trace the templates for the cup and saucer (not the handle) on to the backs of the appropriate fabrics and cut out each piece once, adding a seam allowance of 0.5cm (³/₁₆in) all round. Transfer the pattern arrows as notches in the seam allowances.

2 For the handle, fold a scrap of fabric in half, with right sides together, to make a piece a bit larger than the handle. Place the handle pattern on top and mark on the outlines. Stitch the two curved seams by hand or machine. Trim off the excess fabric, leaving a 0.5cm (³/₁₆in) seam allowance all round, then snip into the allowance for ease and turn the handle out.

3 Pin the cup to the saucer with right sides facing, matching notches. It is easier if you use quite a few pins and it helps to snip into the seam allowance of the saucer too. Stitch the seam and press. Pin the handle to the right of the cup, with the raw edges matching, and sew or tack close to the edge so that nothing can slip.

4 Place the cup on a suitably sized piece of coffee-themed fabric with right sides together (the handle will be between the layers). Place wadding underneath and secure with pins. Sew all round, leaving a small opening at the top for turning. Trim the wadding close to the seam, and trim the fabric on the back to the same size as the front. Cut off the seam allowance at the corners and make snips into it at curves, almost to the stitching. Turn the mug rug out and close up the opening by hand.

5 Draw the rounded line on the saucer freehand with the water-soluble marker pen, and quilt in brown thread. Stitch in the ditch of the seam between the cup and saucer as well.

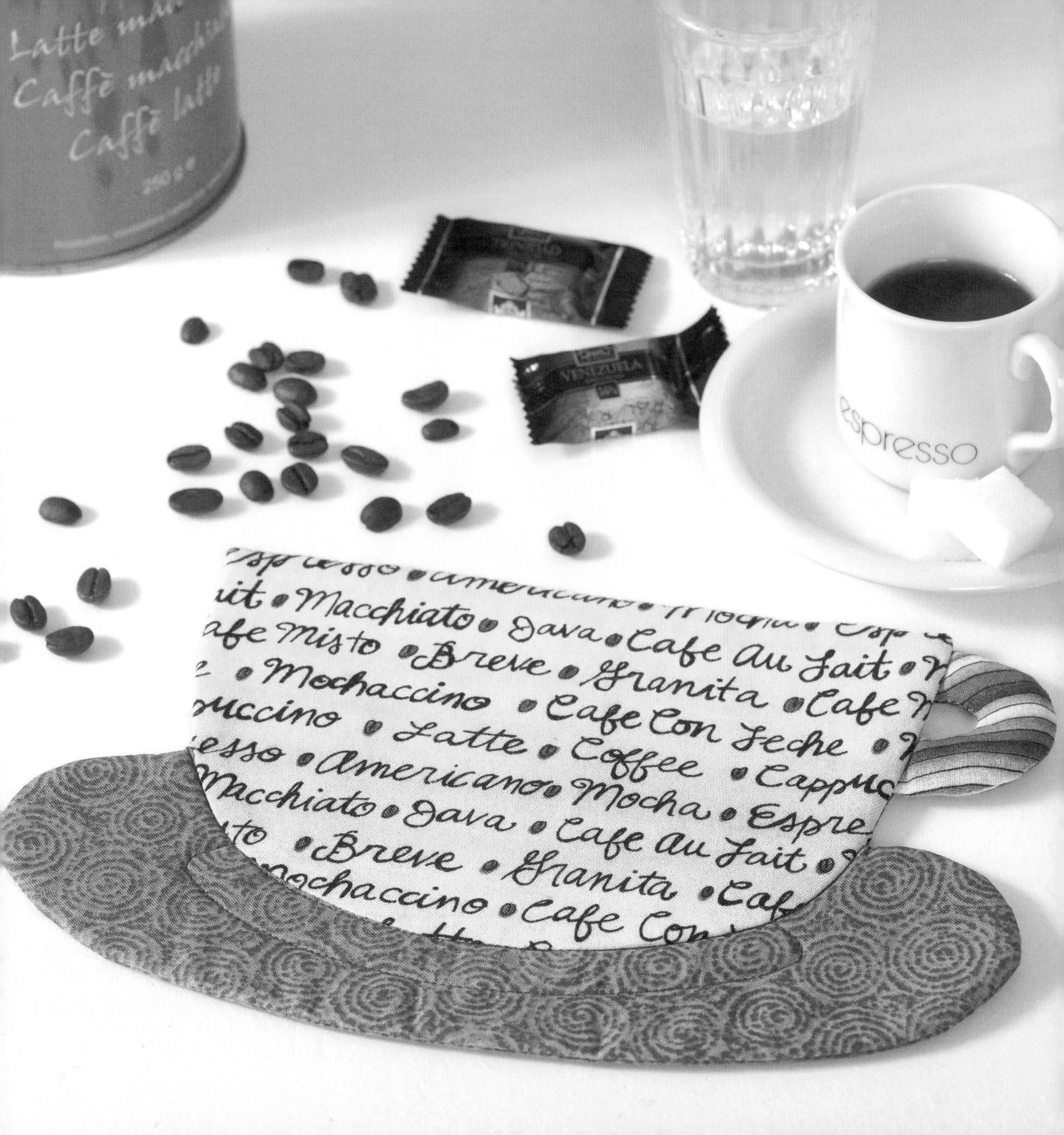
VENEZUELA
espresso

Materials

- 20cm (8in) cream fabric
- 10cm (4in) dark blue fabric
- scraps of blue patterned fabric for the borders
- 20cm (8in) thin fusible interfacing
- 20cm (8in) thin sew-in wadding
- dark blue embroidery cotton
- dark blue quilting thread
- water-soluble marker pen

Cutting out

The following measurements include a 0.75cm (¼in) seam allowance.

- 30 x 20cm (12 x 8in) cream fabric for the embroidery panel
- 26 x 17cm (10¼ x 6¾in) cream fabric for the back
- 4cm (1½in) strips of blue fabric in various lengths and patterns for the borders
- 6.5 x 90cm (2½ x 35½in) dark blue fabric for the binding
- 30 x 20cm (12 x 8in) thin fusible interfacing
- 26 x 17cm (10¼ x 6¾in) sew-in wadding

Transferring the embroidery pattern is easy if you use a light box. The light makes the fabric transparent and the pattern is then simple to trace. Alternatively, tape your pattern and fabric up to a window for the same effect. Textile markers react differently on different fabrics. Please try the marker on a scrap of your fabric first.

Creative Break

Mug rug with embroidered design by Bea Galler

Size: 25.5 x 16.5cm (10 x 6½in)   Pattern 17 on page 61   **Level of difficulty** ♡ ♡

Method

1 Iron the thin fusible interfacing on to the wrong side of the embroidery panel. The interfacing makes the embroidery fabric a little firmer, and prevents the threads from showing through. Using the water-soluble marker, transfer the template so it is centred on the right side of the fabric.

2 Embroider the design using three strands of embroidery cotton, sewing the outlines and words in backstitch, and the line under the words in running stitch. Embroider the flowers in lazy-daisy stitch, then dot the i's and texture the biscuit with French knots (see page 13).

3 Wipe away the marker pen with a damp cloth and press the panel. Trim the panel to 21 x 12cm (8¼ x 4¾in).

4 Join the blue patterned strips on the 4cm (1½in) edges to make a long strip. Cut two pieces 21cm (8¼in) long and attach to the top and bottom of the embroidered panel. Measure the side edges and cut two strips to fit. Attach these and then press all the seams.

5 Pin the front, wadding and back together, right sides out, and quilt by hand just inside the panel seams.

6 Trim the mug rug to 25.5 x 16.5cm (10 x 6½in) and attach the binding using the continuous-binding method (see page 12).

Just a tea and a cookie for a creative break!

Materials

For 3 mug rugs:
- 45cm (17¾in) purple fabric
- 15cm (6in) each of 7 different patterned fabrics in purple, pink and green
- 30cm (12in) wadding
- machine-quilting thread
- rotary cutter and cutting mat

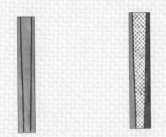

Figure 1   *Figure 2*

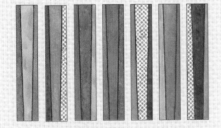

Figure 3

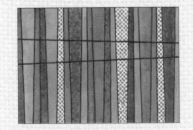

Figure 4

Out of Line

Dynamic trio of mug rugs by Petra Herbrechtsmeier

Size: 21 x 14cm (8¼ x 5½in)   Level of difficulty ♡

Cutting out

A seam allowance of 0.5cm (³/₁₆in) is included.

For 3 mug rugs:
- 7 pieces of patterned fabric 28 x 10cm (11 x 4in)
- 30 x 45cm (12 x 17¾in) purple fabric for the back
- 30 x 45cm (12 x 17¾in) wadding
- 3 pieces of purple fabric 6.5 x 75cm (2½ x 29½in) for the binding

Method

1 Stack the seven pieces for the front on top of each other, right sides up, with edges matching and then press down hard on them with a steam iron.

2 Using a rotary cutter on a cutting mat, cut through the pile of fabrics twice in slightly wonky lines without a ruler – the strips should not be less than 3cm (1¼in) wide. You will have three pieces of each fabric (figure 1).

3 Rearrange the strips to create seven different combinations all forming the original 28 x 10cm (11 x 4in) shape (figure 2). Sew the seven combinations of three fabrics together along the angled edges and press open (figure 3).

4 Place the long sides of the seven segments together, making sure that you do not have two of the same fabrics together. Join the segments together to make a rectangle about 28 x 42cm (11 x 16½in), then cut the rectangle into three pieces freehand in two cuts, making the first cut at least 5cm (2in) from one long edge, and the second cut about 3–5cm (1¼–2in) from the first cut (figure 4).

5 Unpick the first segment of the middle piece and attach it to the other end to offset the colours. Sew the three pieces back together along the long sides (the edges do not have to line up).

6 Pin the pieced front, wadding and back together, right sides out. Quilt spirals on the machine. Cut the quilted fabric into three mug rugs 21 x 14cm (8¼ x 5½in) and bind the edges of each one (see continuous binding, page 12).

Materials

- 20cm (8in) pink checked fabric
- 10cm (4in) pink floral fabric
- 10cm (4in) pink striped fabric
- scraps of pink patterned fabric
- 10cm (4in) fusible webbing
- 20cm (8in) wadding
- 20cm (8in) white crochet trim
- 20cm (8in) pink rickrack braid
- 25cm (10in) green ribbon
- green variegated thread

Cutting out

A seam allowance of 0.75cm (¼in) is included.

- 9.5 x 16cm (3¾ x 6¼in) pink floral fabric for the front side panel
- 14 x 16cm (5½ x 6¼in) pink checked fabric for the main front panel
- 22 x 16cm (8¾ x 6¼in) pink checked fabric for the back
- 22 x 16cm (8¾ x 6¼in) wadding
- 6.5 x 92cm (2½ x 36¼in) pink striped fabric for the edging

Most modern sewing machines have a wide range of embroidery stitches, and they can be used in many different ways – not just to neaten an appliqué, but also as an alternative quilting stitch. Use multicoloured, variegated or contrasting thread for a special effect on plain fabrics to emphasise a seam or provide support for a sewn-on trim.

Nostalgic Charm

Mug rug with appliquéd flower by Renate Bieber

Size: 22 x 16cm (8¾ x 6¼in)   Pattern 18 on page 62   **Level of difficulty** ♡

Method

1 Sew the two front panel pieces together with right sides facing and press the seam open. Draw the flower patterns on to the fusible webbing and cut out, leaving a generous margin all round. Iron the flower and its centre on to the back of the patterned fabric scraps. Cut out the pieces exactly, arrange them on the main front panel and iron to fuse in place. Pin the front, wadding and back together with right sides out.

2 Embroider the edges of the flower and its centre using a decorative machine stitch or work in blanket stitch by hand. Emphasise the seam between the two front pieces with the same stitch. Sew the crochet trim to the seam. Sew the rickrack braid 2.5cm (1in) from the seam using a small machine zigzag. Attach the ribbon 2cm (¾in) from the top edge using a large zigzag or any embroidery stitch on your sewing machine.

3 Edge the mug rug with the pink striped fabric strips using the continuous-binding method (see page 12).

Materials

- ♥ 20cm (8in) white fabric
- ♥ scraps of patterned fabrics in red, green and pink
- ♥ 10cm (4in) green patterned fabric for the hill
- ♥ 10cm (4in) of green striped fabric for the binding
- ♥ 20cm (8in) fusible webbing
- ♥ 20cm (8in) wadding
- ♥ matching thread

Cutting out

A seam allowance of 0.5cm (³/₁₆in) is included.

- ♥ 22 x 15cm (8¾ x 6in) white fabric for the front
- ♥ 24 x 17cm (9½ x 6¾in) white fabric for the back
- ♥ 22 x 5cm (8¾ x 2in) patterned fabric for the hill
- ♥ 2 pieces of green striped fabric 22 x 5.5cm (8¾ x 2¼in) for the top and bottom binding
- ♥ 2 pieces of green striped fabric 20 x 5.5cm (8 x 2¼in) for the side binding
- ♥ 24 x 17cm (9½ x 6¾in) wadding

Plenty of Christmas fabrics appear in the shops every year. If a suitable fabric with printed trees is available, you can cut out the trees and appliqué them on rather than using the tree patterns provided.

Christmas Landscape

Mug rug with Christmas trees by Christa Rolf

Size: 22 x 15cm (8¾ x 6in) Pattern 19 on page 62 **Level of difficulty** ♡ ♡

Method

1 Iron fusible webbing on to the wrong side of the green patterned fabric. Draw a curve on it freehand or use a large dinner or cake plate as a template. (If you want an unsymmetrical hill shape, remember that it will be in mirror image on the right side.) Cut out the hill shape.

2 Trace five trees and their trunks on to the fusible webbing and trace a small star or draw one freehand. Cut out, adding a generous margin all round. Fuse on to the back of your fabric scraps and cut out exactly. Arrange the hill, trees, trunks and star on the front fabric so that the trees and hill overlap the ends of the trunks. Carefully fuse in place.

3 Pin the front, wadding and back together, right sides out. Topstitch close to the edges of the appliqué pieces in matching thread or quilt as desired.

4 Trim the wadding and back fabric to the same size as the front, squaring off the front fabric too, if necessary. Attach the 5.5cm (2¼in) binding strips to the top and bottom and then to the side edges (see page 12).

Templates

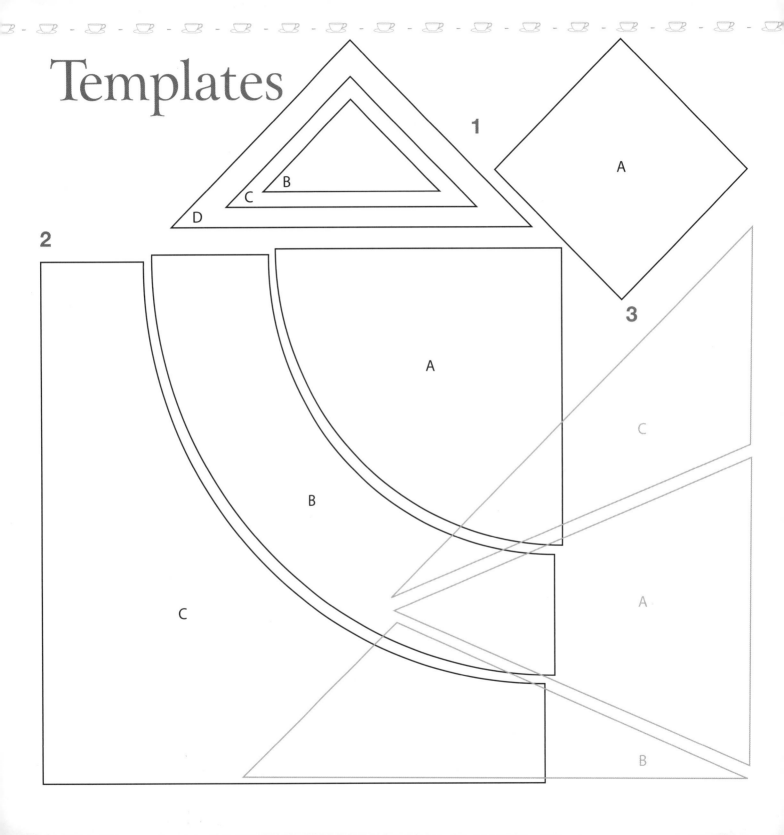

1

B
C
D

A

2

A

B

C

3

C

A

B

4

7

9

Enlarge by 200%

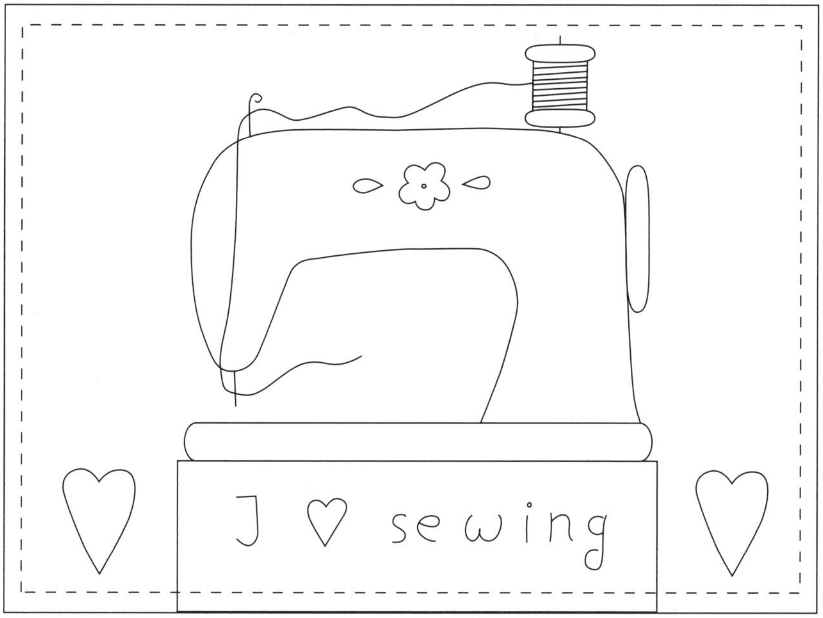

J ♥ sewing

10

16

Enlarge by 200%

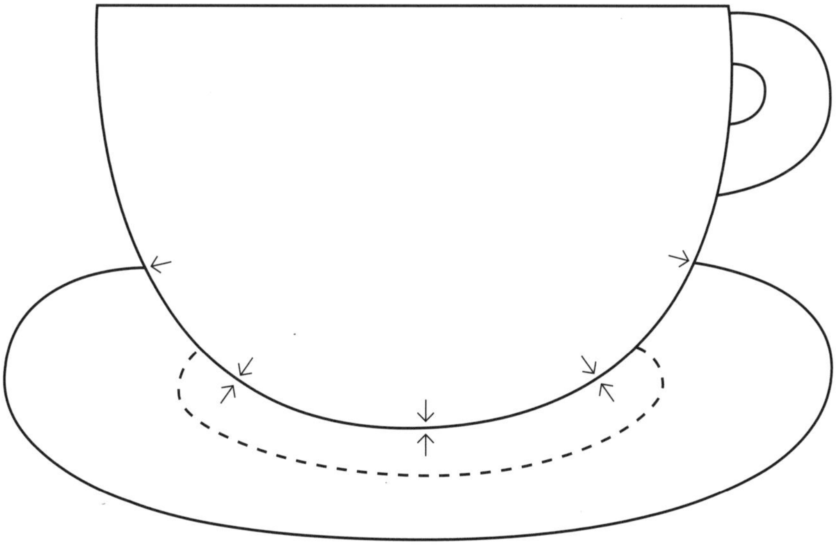

11

15

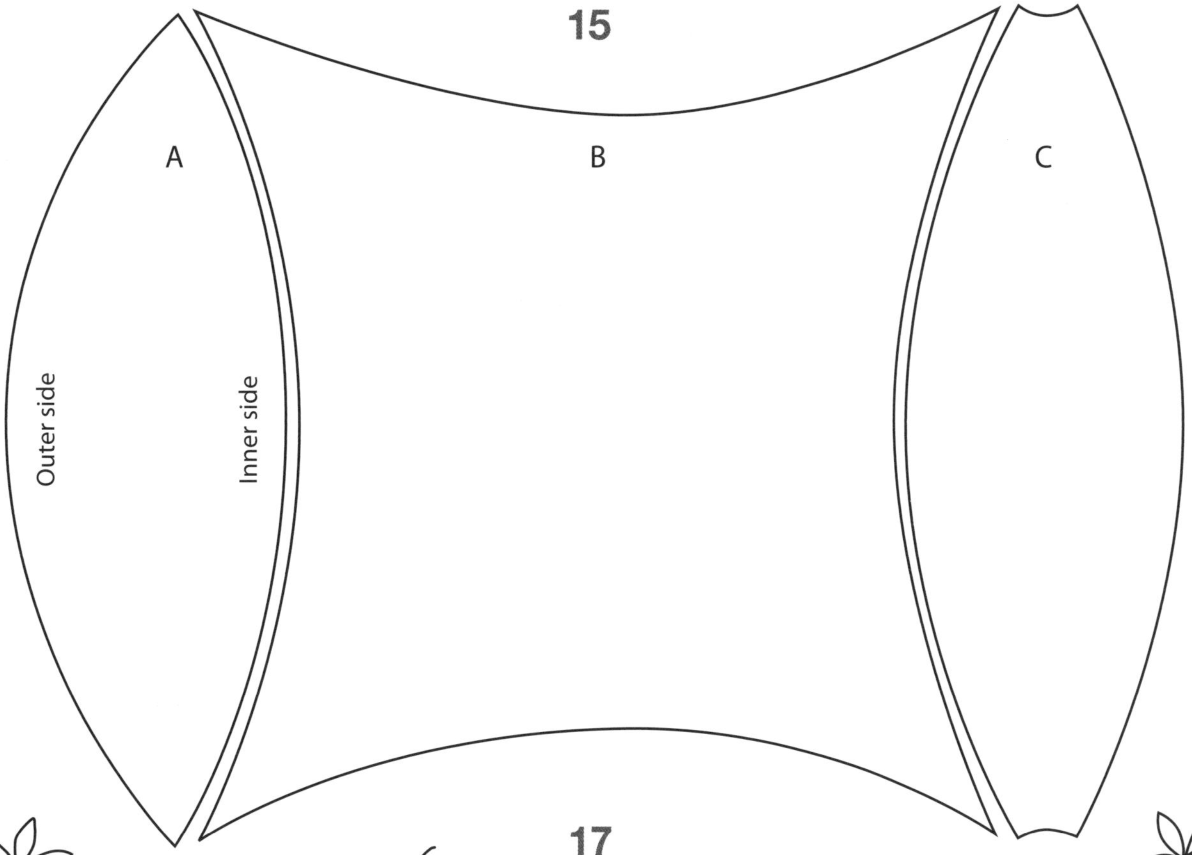

A

Outer side

Inner side

B

C

17

Just a tea and a cookie* for a creative* break!

Manufacturers

The following manufacturers kindly supplied the materials and equipment used by the author. Many of these organisations provide on-line ordering facilities and distribute worldwide. However, all of the materials and equipment used in this book can be readily obtained from alternative sources, including specialist stores, on-line suppliers and mail-order companies.

De Witte Engel, Den Burg, Texel
www.dewitteengel.nl

Freudenberg KG (sale of Vlieseline)
www.vlieseline.de

Frowein
www.kurt-frowein.de

Gütermann AG + Gütermann Sulky, Gutach/Breisgau
www.guetermann.com

Prym-Consumer GmbH, Stolberg
www.prym-consumer.com

Rayher Hobby GmbH, Laupheim
www.rayher-hobby.de

Rinske Stevens Design B.V., Culemborg (NL)
www.dreamboxes.net

Seco Accessoires GmbH, Tirschenreuth
www.seco-knopf.de

Stof A/S, Herning (DK)
www.stof-dk.com

Acknowledgements

The author and publishers are grateful for the models and accessories provided by the following:

Acrylic templates

Quilthaus Hamburg, Andreas Wolf
www.quilthouse.de

Wool felt

Herzquilter, Regine Joskowiak, Dinslaken
www.herzquiltershop.de

Patchwork and accessories

by bea, Beate Mazek, Paderborn
www.bybea.de

Just for Fun, Kerstin Porsch, Ahorn bei Coburg
www.justforfunpatchwork.de

Kinderstoffe Farbenfroh, Beate Pöhlmann, Oberhausen
www.stoffefuerkinder.de